# PICK UP
# AX

D0911343

## *Anthony Clarvoe*

357 W 20th St., NY NY 10011
212 627-1055

PICK UP AX
© Copyright 1990, 1991 Anthony Clarvoe

First printing: November 1991
ISBN: 0-88145-103-7

Book design: Marie Donovan
Word processing: WordMarc Composer Plus
Typographic controls: Xerox Ventura Publisher 2.0 PE
Typeface: Palatino
Printed on recycled acid-free paper, and bound in the USA.

# ABOUT THE AUTHOR

Anthony Clarvoe is co-founder of Upstart Stage in
Berkeley, California. His other plays include THE
REAPPEARING ACT, D.N.R., and SHOW AND
TELL. PICK UP AX was selected by the American
Theater Critics Association for inclusion in
BURNS-MANTLE BEST PLAYS 1989-90. Clarvoe has
received playwriting fellowships from the National
Endowment for the Arts and the Jerome Foundation,
and the Barrie and Bernice Stavis Award as
outstanding emerging playwright of 1990 from the
National Theatre Conference. A San Francisco native,
he lives in the Midwest with his wife, the poet
Jennifer S. Clarvoe.

The writing of PICK UP AX was aided by staged readings at Upstart Stage and in South Coast Repertory's NewSCRipts Series, and through a workshop production by the American Conservatory Theater's Plays in Progress.

PICK UP AX had its mainstage premiere on January 18, 1990, at the Eureka Theatre Company in San Francisco, Suzanne Bennett, Artistic Director, and Debra J. Ballinger, Executive Director. The cast and creative contributors were as follows:

KEITH RIENZI ........................John Bellucci
BRIAN WEISS ....................... Sam Gregory
MICK PALOMAR ......................... Jeff King

*Director* .......................... Susan Marsden
*Set design* ....................David Jon Hoffman
*Lighting* ............................ Jack Carpenter
*Sound* ....................................Pre Pro
*Costumes* ................... Cassandra Carpenter
*Special effects* ........... didi moyse and David Ford

# ACKNOWLEDGMENTS

Of the many people and organizations who helped to create PICK UP AX, the following most particularly influenced the script and deserve my thanks: Padua Hills Playwrights Festival; Dennis Barnett, Carter Lewis, Tom Ramirez, Howard Swain, Chiron Alston, James Carpenter, Ellen Margolis, Upstart Stage; David Emmes, Martin Benson, Jerry Patch, John Glore, Eli Simon, David Esbjornson, South Coast Repertory; Joy Carlin, Arthur Ballet, Jim Lively, American Conservatory Theater; Suzanne Bennett, Susan Marsden, John Bellucci, Sam Gregory, Jeff King, Eureka Theatre Company; Richard E.T. White, Northlight Theatre.

I owe special thanks to David Maier, who directed and designed the American Conservatory Theater Plays in Progress production, and Andrew Dolan, Michael Scott Ryan, and Sam Fontana, who performed it.

My deep gratitude to Jennifer Clarvoe and James Grant Goldin.

Now I'm a man
Way past twenty-one
I want you to believe me, baby
I have lots of fun
*Muddy Waters*

# CHARACTERS

KEITH RIENZI, late 20s. Skinny, with long hair, wearing hightop sneakers, jeans, and a Judas Priest t-shirt except as noted. A well-to-do executive.

BRIAN WEISS, late 20s. A more put-together version of the above: the hair is cut and the shirt has buttons.

MICK PALOMAR, middle 30s. Solid, polished, and corporate, in pinstripes and tie.

# SETTING

Silicon Valley, early 1980s. Many generations in the past.

BRIAN's office: Showpiece desk, chairs, and credenza no one cares about. A beautiful computer workstation. A presentation easel with a big pad of paper and felt pens. Empty walls. Scattered small toys, Transformers, that sort of thing.

# PRODUCTION NOTES

PICK UP AX has been produced in a 50-seat black box, a 500-seat proscenium theatre, and a range of spaces in between. Each production has had its own character, but they have shared a number of discoveries about play:

## THE MOOD ROOM

Times when the set participates in the action are noted in the script. These start with lights and music. As the play goes on and the Mood Room evolves, additional and more intricate activity such as projections, background noise, dry ice, etc. can be excellent.

Some companies have built the Mood Room out of state-of-the-art lighting instruments, banks of slide projectors, and prismatic plastic panels. Others have done it with a couple of sets of strip lights and some scrim. What makes it work are actors who can make believe they are surrended by wonders.

## MUSIC

The heavy metal and other rock and roll mentioned in the script are suggestions for bits and pieces, not complete songs. In production, the most successful playlists have reflected both the characters' moods and Keith and Brian's '70s guitar-hero allegiances.

If you possibly can, use Jimi Hendrix's "Wild Thing" and the Rolling Stones' "Jumping Jack Flash" to end the acts. Trust me on this.

## STYLE

The action is driven by struggles for power fought out through language. Paraphrasing the language confuses the action; relaxing the rhythms relaxes the tension.

The productions thus far have not updated the setting. PICK UP AX is an historical play set in 1980, give or take a year or two. When I wrote about this world, it was already gone. Its stories had become the stuff of legend and its business figures the heroes of a creation myth. That is the perspective from which the play was written and, I think, the one from which it is best performed.

## CHARACTERS

KEITH, despite his rock-and-roll energy, is first and last an intellectual, by which I mean that ideas are the most vivid and passionate beings in the world. "I always knew they were out there, the ideas", is a line about lost love. He learns better than anyone else, and he does so with ruthless concentration.

BRIAN is realizing as the play begins that his success has made him responsible for the welfare of a lot of people. Combined with the threatened loss of a lifetime of work, this realization is a constant, shocking, physical presence, and may be the best

working definition of what it means not to be a kid
anymore.

MICK talks and listens in a way the other two have
never met before. They sometimes say things
ironically, or just for a goof. To MICK, every statement
is an action and a potential threat. He means
everything he says, everything he says is for a reason,
and he expects the same from other adults.

The play seems to work best if BRIAN and KEITH
gradually realize that MICK, despite his corporate
demeanor, is capable of committing an unknown
variety of dangerous acts right now in this room; and,
when it is kept in mind from the very beginning, that
KEITH runs a mean dungeon.

# ACT ONE

## SCENE 1

*(As the house lights go down, we hear Boston's*
Foreplay / Long Time.)

*(*BRIAN *is talking on the phone.* KEITH *is fidgeting with a
toy from the Museum of Modern Art gift shop.)*

BRIAN: *(On phone)*—and I'll go to the media. I'll go
to your other customers. What with? What with, with
my grievances, I'll go to them with this grief you're
giving me. Yes, you, Prescott, you monopoly-
wannabe! Bottleneck, right, you've got a bottleneck,
so what are you doing, tourniquet around mine.
Okay, you do that. And then call me back.

*(*BRIAN *hangs up.)*

KEITH: Anyway.

BRIAN: You may need to know about this.

KEITH: Tell me when you're sure. Anyway. George
is running across this rope bridge, waving the magic
broadsword?

BRIAN: George from Finance? Which character was he?

KEITH: Sven the Berserker.

BRIAN: Oh sure.

KEITH: I set him up good. He runs onto a rope bridge
waving a sharp object, really stupid, even for George.

He slices clean through the support ropes on the bridge. So he's toast.

BRIAN: Oh, sure, you put the bridge troll under that one.

KEITH: Was he surprised.

BRIAN: You run a mean dungeon, Keith. *(The phone rings. He picks it up.)* Yes? Put him through. I'm listening, Prescott. All right, when? We won't be here by then. What relationship? You guys at Mnemonico won't sell me any chips. If you won't take my money, what does our relationship consist of? My money used to be good for you. Okay, so they have bigger money, you can't be satisfied with my size of money anymore? I want to see you. I want to talk to you. Not productive, don't tell me productive, what do you produce? Produce something I can buy, make my product out of, get my ass back in the food chain. We'll talk. *(Slams phone, picks it up again, pushes two buttons.)* He's not budging. Okay. I want to meet with the heads of the following corporations: call Andy at Omnibyte, Howie at Imagicron, Pete at Infodyne, and Fred at Fredco. They're all getting squeezed the same as us. God, you're right. God. All right, then, we tell the board of directors—

BRIAN and KEITH: The shitheads!

*(BRIAN presses two buttons.)*

BRIAN: Goddamn flock of albatrosses better start flapping its wings. Marketing? He's not budging. Set up a press conference. The theme? The theme is we're the one growth industry left in America and we're getting strangled in our cradle by the snakes we rely on for our raw materials just when we're standing the goddamn economy on its punchdrunk legs again! So phrase it how you want. Transfer me to Legal. No, I'll wait.

KEITH: I bet I could get all his credit cards cancelled. You want me to? I could find him in here, *(Patting his terminal)* have him buy imaginary stuff, send him past his limits?

BRIAN: Keith, maybe you'd better go back to your office.

KEITH: I can't.

BRIAN: Why not?

KEITH: It's full.

BRIAN: Full of what?

KEITH: This and that. I filled it up.

BRIAN: It's a room, not a disk drive. *(Into phone)* Hi, yeah, he's not budging. What does the Justice Department say? Yeah? Then Justice is a fucking misnomer. Can we get a restraining order? Sure I know what a restraining order is, you're here to tell me. Try it. *(BRIAN hangs up.)* Keith, listen.

*(KEITH quickly puts his head down on the desk, ear to the surface.)*

KEITH: Many buffalo, Kemosabe.

BRIAN: Keith—

KEITH: 132,982 buffalo, Kemosabe.

BRIAN: You know I try to keep this shit away from you. But you'll read it off the networks anyway. *(KEITH sits up, surprised.)* We're in real trouble this time.

KEITH: What you mean— *(BRIAN joins in.)*

KEITH and BRIAN: —we, white man.

BRIAN: Microchips. Supply can't keep up with demand—remember I explained how that works? Mnemonico will only sell chips to the big boys. I can't

win a bidding war with them. I think the big boys
want to put us little boys out of business, and the
chip makers are helping them.

KEITH: I don't get it.

BRIAN: Dude? No hardware, no product. No product,
no company.

KEITH: But I hate hardware!

BRIAN: You heard me calling Andy and Howie and
Pete and Fred?

KEITH: Those guys are all great Dungeons and
Dragons players! I haven't played them for years.

BRIAN: This is a new game. Everybody's got his own
corporation now, but together we can beat the big
boys.

KEITH: I used to be on the network half the night with
those guys.

BRIAN: Now the time is right to go networking in the
street.

KEITH: You know, if everything were networked,
I could really function. I never should have strayed
from pure programming.

BRIAN: Keith, we had to, you know we did. Your stuff
was too smart for the standard machines.

KEITH: I would die of happiness if I could design
software that didn't need any hardware.

BRIAN: They have that already. It's called "thought."

KEITH: I'm tied forever to a cross of silicon. The
computers' last tie to the goddamn world of matter.

BRIAN: Don't knock the world of matter, it's where
we sell your ideas. Every time we have a crisis do you
have to write off the whole material world?

KEITH: What's it done for us lately? Look at what's left of you.

BRIAN: Keith, listen to me. Without the world of matter, there would be no Rolling Stones.

KEITH: Okay. You have a point.

BRIAN: All I'm saying is reconcile yourself—

KEITH: *(Tapping at the terminal)* I'm trying. Hey, I have a surprise for you.

BRIAN: —use it to your advantage.

KEITH: It's an old idea I dug up. Move two feet to your left.

(BRIAN *does so. Grand Funk Railroad's* We're an American Band *starts up, low.)*

BRIAN: What's going on?

KEITH: You break the plane, the sensors read your vital signs. Digitize your mood. You like it?

BRIAN: Sympathetic Muzak. Cute.

KEITH: See, I listen to you. I try to meet the world halfway. You want to go out tonight? We could get stoned and play miniature golf?

*(Blackout)*

## SCENE 2

*(The walls have turned a cold shade of blue.* KEITH *is at the computer.* BRIAN *enters.)*

KEITH: Someone said you were in the newspapers.

BRIAN: "Industry Held Hostage." Didn't help. What have you done to my walls?

KEITH: It's supposed to be soothing.

BRIAN: Makes you look a little dead, load.

(KEITH *looks up at* BRIAN *and punches a few keys.
The lights change.* KEITH *turns back to the screen.*)

BRIAN: Every one of the goddamn board of directors—

KEITH and BRIAN: The shitheads!

BRIAN: —all they did was ask how we got into this
crisis. So much for clout. I'm down to stems and
seeds. We're going to have to slow production.
Lay off some people. Do you want to help? Can we
announce that you're working on something new?
That would buy us some time.

KEITH: *(Pointing to his own head, wearily)* I've got bugs
in this machine.

BRIAN: I held off telling you as long as I—

KEITH: Always now there's white noise in my head:
crisis crisis crisis. My medium is electrons in
suspension. You interrupt the power for a fraction of
a second, everything vanishes. Remember when we
gave that grant to the Exploratorium?

BRIAN: I'm with you.

KEITH: When I went up for the check-passing pictures
I wandered around, and they had this exhibit. A long
tray of soapy water on the floor, and out of it you
hoist a horizontal bar on wires. And the bar across the
top and the wires down the sides and the surface of
the soapy water on the bottom made a frame for a
sheet of the stuff that bubbles are.

BRIAN: Rad.

KEITH: It hung in front of you and you could see
yourself in it. And behind you this grungy museum.
And everything like you're made out of rainbows.
If somebody stood on the other side of it, you could
see them too, like you were mixed together in

suspension. But the sheet of suds would get too heavy for its own weight, and it would blink away. And you'd be gone and the room would be gone and the liquid prism effect was gone and all there was was the person on the other side of a tray of soap. Looking really mundane.

BRIAN: Keith? You okay?

KEITH: I was in meetings till late yesterday. This kid made a presentation. *(He waves a piece of paper covered with calculations. On and off during the following, almost unconsciously, he folds it into an odd-looking paper airplane.)*

BRIAN: One of the new kids?

KEITH: One of the new new kids. Summer intern.

BRIAN: How was it?

KEITH: We'd given him a little something. He was at the chalkboard. He was talking. He'd gone way above and beyond. And I was following him. I was following what he was saying.

BRIAN: Great, so?

KEITH: He was retracing his line of thought and I was following. Along. Behind him.

BRIAN: Oh.

KEITH: Right. When have I ever had to follow anybody through the numbers? I'm always blindsiding them and running on ahead.

BRIAN: You were tired. It was late.

KEITH: I came back here. I worked all night.

BRIAN: Like the old days.

KEITH: The old days weren't work, so much. I'd look up, it'd be hours later, like flying across the time zones. And I'd brought back all this stuff on disk.

BRIAN: I've seen you going after ideas.

KEITH: They came to me. You saw me opening my arms, that's all. Last night I was running after it.

BRIAN: Meanwhile the kid went out with his friends, and they bought him a pitcher, and they told him he was going to be the next Keith Rienzi, and a few beers later he believed them, and somebody drove him home and he looked in the bathroom mirror and said, "I am the next Keith Rienzi." And all this time Keith Rienzi was back here working. The once and future kid.

KEITH: You know, I'm twenty-seven years old. That's fifty-four in nerd years.

(KEITH *breathes on one wing of his airplane, making it slightly heavier to cause the plane to bank.* KEITH *flies the paper airplane across the room.*)

BRIAN: He had the element of surprise this time. That won't happen again.

KEITH: No. I'll be looking over my shoulder. That's always productive. What I design almost doesn't exist at all. Hardware, now, you're in the world of wires and boards and trays. Bound for the junkyard. With software, cathedrals of logic vanish into the ozone. In a twinkling.

BRIAN: I'd say you're still thinking.

KEITH: I'm remembering thinking. If I were really thinking I wouldn't have to say these things.

*(Pause)*

BRIAN: Here's what we do. First of all for God's sake don't tell anyone, our stock will go to hell. We'll pull you out of everything. Global erase, okay? R and D management, new product oversight, everything. We'll say what I was talking about before: Keith Rienzi is working on something new, and screw your old memory chips.

KEITH: Can I move in here?

BRIAN: Of course. You have a nightmare, you head for Mom and Dad's room. We'll take you out of yourself and things'll come back to you.

KEITH: That's it, that's how it was. They'd come right out of the dark. I always knew they were out there, the ideas.

(KEITH *taps a few keys and waits for a program to boot up.*)

BRIAN: That's my boy. (BRIAN *comes around to read over* KEITH's *shoulder.*) "You are standing in a forest clearing near a small stone cottage...." Keith, you're playing Adventure?

KEITH: Different game, same idea. It's where I used to get away to think.

BRIAN: Exploring an imaginary maze?

KEITH: Some people pace.

BRIAN: Okay, whatever breaks you out of the slump.

(*Pause*)

KEITH: What if I don't?

BRIAN: Hey. This place is our life's work. It owes you.

KEITH: You try it.

BRIAN: I've hated this stupid pastime since high school.

KEITH: You'll get it one of these days. Every time they kill you, you get right up again. Come on, it's highly educational.

BRIAN: Educational, if we did business with swords, I'd learn all kinds of useful stuff.

KEITH: Help me, Obi-wan Kenobi, you're my only hope. Help me, Obi-wan Kenobi, you're my only hope. Help me, Obi-wan—

BRIAN: Keith! I'm in a crisis here! Okay. Maybe I haven't made it clear. This company, legally, is a person. Right? A character, like in Dungeons and Dragons? Out there, other people are fighting our character. Hack and slash. They're trying to kill it, and if they do, it'll never get up again. *(Pause)* So I need your help. I've got to try everything. Okay? If anyone asks the question, what do you say?

KEITH: Brian is trying everything. How's your stomach?

BRIAN: Don't mention my stomach.

KEITH: Brian is trying everything.

BRIAN: How often do kids like us get this far? Come on.

KEITH: Never.

BRIAN: Who's gonna stake us to a second chance?

KEITH: Nobody. I thought we had money of our own by now.

BRIAN: Only on paper. If the company dies, you and I and your bright ideas go on down to scrapheap town. Now do you see where we are?

KEITH: We are standing in a forest clearing near a small stone cottage.

*(Pause. BRIAN looks at the screen.)*

BRIAN: "You are standing in a forest clearing near a small stone cottage. Suddenly a dwarf carrying a stone ax runs out of the woods. He drops the stone ax, opens the cottage door, runs through, and slams the door." Okay. Go through door?

KEITH: You sure you want to do that?

BRIAN: I hate it when you say that! Leave forest clearing, go to Taco Bell? I don't know.

KEITH: What do you have?

BRIAN: A clearing, a cottage, a door, a disappeared dwarf.

KEITH: A stone ax.

BRIAN: Aha. Pick up stone ax.

KEITH: It doesn't know "pick up." Try "get."

BRIAN: You see? Complex, exotic, pathetically limited. "Get stone ax. Enter." Okay. "The stone ax says, 'Command me, O Master.'" Now we're happening.

*(Blackout)*

## SCENE 3

*(Lights up on the empty office. MICK enters, expecting to find someone there. He stands in the middle of the room. Behind him, the walls turn burning orange. Led Zeppelin's* Rock and Roll *bursts on at maximum volume. MICK swiftly spins and crouches. When no attackers come, he straightens up and waits for an explanation.)*

*(BRIAN and KEITH enter. Everyone has to speak at a shout.)*

MICK: I'm looking for the office of the president!

BRIAN: This is it!

MICK: Yeah? I have an appointment!

BRIAN: With who? *(Robert Plant's voice drowns out MICK's.)* Keith! Kill the music!

(KEITH *pushes a button on his computer. The music goes off. The walls of the room return to neutral.*)

MICK: Mr. Weiss? Mr. Rienzi?

BRIAN: Yes.

KEITH: Present.

MICK: Good morning. My name is Mick Palomar.

BRIAN: Sorry about the—

KEITH: I'll have to work that out.

MICK: I've been following your crisis.

BRIAN: Palomar? I don't recognize—

MICK: I'm not from electronics. I've been hearing your story in the media. I thought my experience might lend you some perspective. You should have gotten my materials.

BRIAN: We may have. We're not great believers in paper.

MICK: Neither am I. I'm more of a hands-on guy.

KEITH: Listen, dudes, don't mind me here, I'm going to divide my attention.

MICK: Mr. Rienzi, are the walls changing color?

BRIAN: We're sitting in the prototype of Keith Rienzi's latest inspiration. Everything here is in R and D. Research and Development. You remember mood rings? This is a mood room.

KEITH: Yeah! I like that!

BRIAN: The computer picks up changes in your system and converts them to output. We feel your office should enable you to resonate.

MICK: It'll tell you what you're feeling?

BRIAN: That's the idea. Right now it's like being trapped in a psychotic jukebox, but we'll get it.

MICK: I appreciate your telling me. I'm not used to Led Zeppelin in a business context.

KEITH: He can stay. Brian, you know, a building full of offices like this, or a labyrinth of cubicles, all in motion, each with a different character, it would be like—think about it—it could be like Dungeons and Dragons. It could be this paradise.

BRIAN: Keith....

MICK: See, this is how I'd pictured a growth corporation.

BRIAN: What's your background?

MICK: Heavy industry.

BRIAN: *(Prompting)* So you've heard we're in a shakeout, companies falling right and left....

MICK: That says you're happening. Two years from now, the ones left standing will be standing solid. You guys look promising.

KEITH: We don't feel very promising today.

MICK: That's where perspective comes in. What you need is a troubleshooter.

BRIAN: I don't have a lot of spare time for consultations and agonizing reappraisal of my top management.

MICK: I agree. I'm more of a hands-on guy. We do some brainstorming, how about it?

BRIAN: Look, Mr. Palomar, every idea I've had I've done.

KEITH: Brian is trying everything.

MICK: I'll have some new ideas. May I restate your problem? You're getting squeezed by your key supplier. The company's name is Mnemonico. The man in charge is named Prescott.

BRIAN: I've shouted this into every microphone in sight. I know this.

MICK: Here's what no one knows. *(Taking a piece of paper from his pocket)* This is the list of all the companies buying chips from Mnemonico. All the under-the-table deals.

BRIAN: That isn't public. How did you get it?

MICK: That isn't important. The information is important.

*(MICK hands the paper to BRIAN.)*

BRIAN: *(Stunned)* Andy...Howie...Pete...Fred...

KEITH: We know these guys.

BRIAN: I thought I knew these guys. We held meetings. We held a press conference. I stood side by side in public with these people. Denouncing under-the-table deals. They had me be the—the spokesman. Oh, I get the idea. I get it now. I always suspected this was how people were, down deep. *(Blinking back tears)* I still have the blue spots in my eyes, from squinting into camera lights and spouting about fair play. Like a fool.  Am I the only martyr? Does everybody have a deal but me?

MICK: Just the fast learners. And the multinationals.

BRIAN: The big boys. The fast learners and the big boys.

MICK: So. Now you know where you are.

BRIAN: Not on the list.

KEITH: Brian. You tried everything.

BRIAN: Evidently not.

(MICK *goes to easel.)*

MICK: The question is: What does Mnemonico want from you?

BRIAN: Nothing. I've talked myself dry. We have nothing they want.

MICK: Are you going under?

BRIAN: They don't care. What do you do when they don't care?

MICK: Something they won't like.

(MICK *flips to a blank page on the easel pad and picks up a big felt-tip pen.)*

BRIAN: I mobilized the other companies—the fucks! I called the lawyers, I've had it all over the press. The public is outraged. Letters to the Editor, speeches in the Assembly.

MICK: Your reasoning has been sound. You've tried to get him where he lives. Taken in order:

(MICK *writes "Self-Image.")*

KEITH: *(Trying to guess as* MICK *writes)* Self...Image.

MICK: You've tried to paint Mr. Prescott as an evil businessman. And embarrassment can be an excellent tool.

BRIAN: Unethical bastard didn't mind.

MICK: No, he didn't. It's going to be an unethical decade. He's got the jump on you toughnesswise.

(MICK *writes "Reputation.")*

KEITH: Reputation.

MICK: You tried, through the press, to destroy his reputation.

BRIAN: Did I do that?

MICK: Oh, yeah. Libellous, maybe. It hasn't worked because all you're saying is that he's got too much leverage, and business people know that there's no such thing as too much leverage. Do you own a dog?

BRIAN: I don't have time.

MICK: Neither do I. My daughters do. You want to learn about leverage? Go to the park, watch the dogs. Three dogs, strangers to each other, they play for a minute and they have a hierarchy. Doesn't take bloodshed for a dog to work out who gets to do the humping. That's what leverage does. There are other ways—

(MICK *writes "Blackmail."*)

KEITH: Blackmail.

BRIAN: What do we do, film him in a hotel room with a hooker?

MICK: Not really—

KEITH: It would be the greatest day of his life.

BRIAN: Let's pass on that.

MICK: —I'm making a point. *(Above the other words,* MICK *writes "Relationships.")* The tactics you've used are all ways to threaten his relationships. A sound idea, but we can explore other—

BRIAN: Sue them!

(MICK *writes "Law."*)

MICK: Force Mnemonico through the courts. Now, lawsuits, as you know, are slow. Have you had any luck legally? Antitrust and so on?

BRIAN: They seem to be within their goddamn rights.

MICK: If you do go under, you can sue for revenge, but—

KEITH: We could use a little revenge.

BRIAN: Justice.

MICK: Memory chips. At this stage, do you want your chips or your revenge? You may get only one.

BRIAN: Okay, so tell me. What do they care about?

MICK: Mnemonico has needs, just as you do— (MICK *writes "Needs."*) and sources to supply them. Start with the basics. Staying alive and healthy....

BRIAN: Obviously.

MICK: Never overlook the obvious.

KEITH: Break his legs!

BRIAN: Serious up, okay?

(MICK *writes "Break his legs."*)

MICK: This is brainstorming. Everything goes in.

BRIAN: Let's leave that aside for a moment.

MICK: What else do they value? Their security.

(MICK *writes "Supplies."*)

KEITH: Supplies.

MICK: There are ways to cut off his raw materials. These take time and resources.

KEITH: Are you talking about sabotage?

MICK: No.

(MICK *writes "Sabotage."*)

MICK: Sabotage.

BRIAN: Guys, look, I'd just like to find a better way to talk to him.

MICK: How do you mean?

BRIAN: Talk to him. Sit down with him, reasonably, present the case for cooperation being in the best interest of both parties, search for a mutually satisfactory compromise. Talk to him. You know.

MICK: Sure.

(MICK *writes "Talk", very small.*)

BRIAN: And if that doesn't work, have him killed.

(MICK *keeps writing: "Kill him."*)

KEITH: Now you're talking.

BRIAN: It's a joke.

MICK: Goes without saying. A little healthy release. (MICK *draws a smiley face next to "Kill him."*) Okay, one idea you haven't mentioned. It may be new to you. Appeal to the people that make the corporation. Find the weak link in the chain of command. Appeal to that person's financial needs.

(MICK *writes "Bribery."*)

KEITH and BRIAN: Bribery.

MICK: Have you tried bribing anyone?

BRIAN: Not me. I wouldn't know the first thing about bribing someone.

MICK: You're a middle-class American, no one expects you to know that stuff. What do we need? Can we get by with what bounces off the forklift?

BRIAN: No, we're talking truckloads.

MICK: To the top, then. I thought as much. You want to know why I think this is happening? This man Prescott. I believe the big fish are bribing him to sell only to them, and the small fry are bribing him to let them buy anyway. Mr. Prescott is Lucky Pierre.

*(Pause)* I can take care of this for you. I can feel this man out. I can talk to some of the other clowns, find out who's slipping what to whom. And you can stay here in paradise.

BRIAN: And in return?

MICK: What I want at this point is to make my bones for you guys. This business—the electronic business. You're a growth industry. Maybe the only one.

BRIAN: Heavy industry is heading overseas, isn't it?

MICK: Or up in smoke. Yeah. My fees are extremely negotiable.

*(Pause)*

BRIAN: Talk to him.

MICK: All right. And report back to you?

BRIAN: Yes. Sure. *(MICK exits. KEITH pushes buttons on the computer. The walls change color and Kansas's* Carry On, Wayward Son *starts up, low.)* Hey, Frodo?

KEITH: What is it, Sam?

BRIAN: Was he your appointment?

KEITH: My appointment? I thought he was your appointment.

*(Blackout)*


## SCENE 4

*(KEITH stares at the computer screen, singing Pink Floyd's* Comfortably Numb *under his breath.)*

KEITH: Hello, hello, hello, is there anybody in there?...

*(BRIAN enters.)*

BRIAN: Keith? There is nothing on the screen.

KEITH: I can see the numbers.

BRIAN: The only thing on the screen is your reflection.

KEITH: I'm trying to think them.

(MICK *enters.*)

MICK: You free?

BRIAN: Come in.

MICK: Man, it's hot out there.

BRIAN: You're burning up. Don't all the offices have air conditioning?

MICK: Out there. Out of doors?

BRIAN: Oh, there.

MICK: I saw the guy in his office, but first I went by his house.

BRIAN: You went to his house?

MICK: Doesn't anybody in this company do legwork?

KEITH: We mostly stick by our terminals. I'll just—

MICK: Get some sunshine, learn a lot.

(KEITH *exits.*)

MICK: I talked with him.

BRIAN: What did he say?

MICK: He said shit. He spewed the typical pathological shit on me. The allotments are set, blah blah blah, there are many criteria, blah blah blah. I reasoned with the man.

BRIAN: What happened with the bribe?

MICK: Not much. I'd seen his house. It's away up in the hills, a few more years above the smog line. He thought. Place is an electronic showroom. Dishes, antennas, looks like a listening post. It's your boy

Keith's dream palace. And it's all bribes. I checked on his income.

BRIAN: You're kidding. You're not a hacker, are you?

MICK: Like on computers? Nah, I still talk to people. I found out about the guy. Legit salary, talking pittance. But the man is living under the table.

BRIAN: This fucking industry.

MICK: Happens all over.

BRIAN: So why can't we bribe him too?

MICK: You're full of questions. A bribe and it's love all around. There's already too much love in his lifestyle. For a jackass like this, there is the carrot or there is the stick. He's been eating carrots from the big boys. Your carrot will not turn him around. Which leaves us with the stick.

(MICK *crosses to the easel, picks up a pen, and slashes lines through "Talk", "Bribery", "Reputation", etc. The only options left are "Break his legs", "Sabotage", and "Kill him.")*

MICK: This is where you are.

BRIAN: What do you mean by "stick"?

MICK: Nothing, if you prefer. Absolutely nothing. I'll tell you anything you need to know.

BRIAN: That's not the way we work.

MICK: I think we agree that the way you work now is not working.

BRIAN: There are things we could be doing better.

MICK: I agree. One of those things is making your presence felt. Especially by this man, who is clearly not a person.

BRIAN: He's a walking talking force of injustice.

MICK: And he's boning you bloody. He deserves for someone to have him hurt.

BRIAN: I don't want anything physical going on.

MICK: Who said physical? Did I say physical?

BRIAN: You just told me you were going to hurt him.

MICK: I said he deserves to be hurt.

BRIAN: Whatever.

MICK: There is all the difference. There is hurting and hurting. Do you really think I would actually, say for example, have someone's fingers broken? And tell you about it?

BRIAN: I don't know.

MICK: No, no, no, the day I come to you and say I'm going to hurt somebody, you should relax, knowing by definition I won't be literally physically busting him up.

BRIAN: What are you planning to do?

MICK: Didn't I just get through explaining?

(BRIAN *makes a rumbling "urp".*)

MICK: You okay?

BRIAN: I'm okay. I've got this indigestion thing. This never happened when I was younger.

MICK: Younger, Jesus, you still got training wheels to me.

BRIAN: I don't want anybody beaten up over this, okay?

MICK: Now wait now wait now wait. Where is that coming from? Okay, that's inexperience, running your mouth. You're thinking in extremes.

BRIAN: I'm raising a moral point. It's a question of ethics.

MICK: One: Forgive me for saying I know the ethics of this arena. The world of leverage is my particular arena. Two: You know the expression "History is written by the winners"? Ethics is written by the losers.

BRIAN: Nice guys finish last. This is like sports, isn't it?

MICK: Nice guys don't even start. Which may be why I don't know any nice guys. You've come pretty far. Is this from nice?

BRIAN: Maybe I'm maturing.

MICK: Maybe you are. Maybe you're looking for an excuse?

(KEITH *enters. He takes a step back.*)

KEITH: Sorry, I'll come back.

MICK: Stick around. Learn about your business.

KEITH: I'm definitely gone.

BRIAN: Keith isn't the businessman.

MICK: You're a corporate officer. This is the office of the president of a corporation.

KEITH: It is? Oh, my God! Somebody do something! (KEITH *pushes a button. Derek and the Dominos's* Layla *comes on, loud.*) The air guitars, men! Hurry!

(KEITH *and* BRIAN *jump up and play air guitar. The walls pulsate in colors.* MICK *watches for a while, bemused, then shrugs and strolls toward the door. He pauses inadvertently in the plane of the mood room sensors. Systems overload. Over the speakers blares a fight to the death between rock and roll and big-band swing. A big spotlight hits the grinning* MICK, *lip-synching to the voice of Frank Sinatra.*)

MICK: Guys! This place is fabulous!

(MICK *sings along, arms wide.* KEITH *and* BRIAN *stare in amazement.*)

(*Blackout*)

## SCENE 5

(MICK *is watching* BRIAN.)

BRIAN: I keep thinking if only I were smarter.
Come up with another idea.

MICK: You're more than smart enough.

BRIAN: There's smart and there's smart. Why did you
leave heavy industry?

MICK: I wanted to see more of my daughters. How
they turn out. You guys don't have a lot of street
smarts, I'll say that.

BRIAN: We didn't need it. We made an early killing.
Three years ago we were in a cinderblock
outbuilding. Total garage band. You bumped into
the wall, it took the skin right off you. We didn't even
have insulation. Now we've got climate control.

MICK: The shakeout is underway. Now the real killing
starts.

BRIAN: The computer was a machine for making
money. Back then all you needed was a bright idea.

MICK: Or someone you knew with a bright idea. Your
buddy Keith's got no street in him at all, does he?

BRIAN: He's a major stockholder in a multimillion-
dollar company. He's not a complete bubblehead.
He knows every number in the world personally.
38 cubed, nice to see you, four to the tenth, how's
it hangin'. But you put a dollar sign in front of a

number, it's like this mask in front of its face. If it's a number of dollars, he's a stranger. I tried.

MICK: So he doesn't need any street. He's the genius boy. Where do you come in?

BRIAN: I've got some street. Sort of suburban street. People ask if it's an equal partnership. Have you ever seen Keith type? Frightening. Reflexes like an animal— if an antelope had hands, you know?

MICK: Are you saying you're his keeper, or—?

BRIAN: Maybe. His trainer. We met over videogames. Late one night, Silverball Palace. I see this crowd at one machine like they're—well, at Marine World, okay? Oohing and aahing at this kid. Women even, a couple of them together, Led Zep t-shirts and jeans. Heaven. I said, "Good, isn't he? You want to smoke a joint with us when he finishes?" And they go, "Bitchin'!" So I whipped out to Telegraph, scored a bag, whipped back up. Keith's beaten the machine record ten times over and his skinny little arms are tired, so he turns around and I'm all over him going, "Hi I'm Brian—what's your name again?—I got a couple of girls over there—See the girls?—They want to meet you, let's go to the parking lot." So here's Keith, in the parking lot, with women. And he's looking at me like I'm the one with miracle reflexes. I came up out of nowhere and gave him a life.

MICK: You score?

BRIAN: I sucked face with one girl, he and the other one sort of looked at each other. He wrote her letters for a year. So like I say, sort of suburban street. But that's the street where Keith lives.

MICK: You boys are about to get urbanized. You're face to the wall and the broomsticks are getting close.

You turn around or you take what comes. Those are the only options I see.

BRIAN: I liked this industry. Yeah, there's a few giants, and they act like giants. But the real clout is a bright idea. If it starts to be muscle, where does it stop? *(Pause)* I was afraid this would happen.

MICK: I like you guys. Don't tell me you're afraid.

BRIAN: No, not like that, I mean—

MICK: Okay. You're afraid. I appreciate your speaking to me frankly. I'll be frank back to you. You're a young man.

BRIAN: I know.

MICK: But you're living in the past. The ones that fall, they're going to fall out of fear. They'll be afraid of what'll become of them. So they curl up and die.

BRIAN: I'm cold. Is it cold in here?

MICK: I've been outside.

BRIAN: *(Glancing toward the sensors)* It must be another one of Keith's ideas. *(Pause)* He called me. Prescott.

MICK: Oh, yeah?

BRIAN: He said you lost your temper.

MICK: Great, he bought that? All right. I got to him.

BRIAN: It sounds like you may have alienated him some.

MICK: He thought I'd really lost it, huh? God, what an industry.

BRIAN: You weren't really pissed?

MICK: Of course I was pissed, but I didn't lose my temper. I didn't lose shit. Good negotiator never gets out of control. What I went in wanting was for him to think I had this dangerous temper.

BRIAN: You succeeded. He said you were a pig.

MICK: He said what?

BRIAN: He said that you had acted like a pig.

MICK: Get it right, now. Be sure.

BRIAN: That's what he said, he said who's this cowboy working for you, he's coming in here acting like a pig.

MICK: Pig. He said pig.

BRIAN: That was the specific animal.

MICK: I'm gonna hurt him. A man—a man cannot accept this leech. Our company, with as little growth as there is in the world, and he calls me a pig. To my employer. Oh, no. This is personal. This is me now. I've got a fucking M.B.A.! I come here— *(Pause)* Why'd you tell me this?! *(Pause)* You don't know how it ties my hands.

BRIAN: This isn't heavy industry.

MICK: I thought I'd put those days behind me, but I guess those days are here. All right. I no longer feel the need to be civilized.

*(Pause)*

BRIAN: Do what you think best.

*(*MICK *gives* BRIAN *a long, appraising look, and exits.)*

*(Blackout)*

*(Def Leppard's* Pour Some Sugar on Me*)*

## SCENE 6

(BRIAN *is sitting at his desk, staring into space.* KEITH *flies in.*)

KEITH: This building is really constricting, you know? Why haven't I noticed it before? Brian? No one is sitting in that chair.

BRIAN: Sorry?

KEITH: You're making eye contact with a void. I've got to get out of here. You want to do some videos? Try this. All-night movies: *The Man Who Fell to Earth, The Hunger,* and *Merry Christmas, Mr. Lawrence.* A David Bowie film festival.

BRIAN: And as the sun comes up we shoot ourselves. It's an option. Should we get some other people?

KEITH: *The Hunger's* got Catherine Deneuve and Susan Sarandon, right?

BRIAN: Yeah.

KEITH: What other people would we want?

BRIAN: Live people, I'm thinking.

KEITH: *(Apprehensive)* Oh, sure. Company.

BRIAN: Some of the kids from Software Design?

KEITH: I'm seeing them in my sleep.

BRIAN: You want to double date?

KEITH: I don't want to scrabble through my brain for conversation.

BRIAN: How many times have I told you: All you have to do is ask them questions, they'll do the talking. You learn stuff that'll peel your paint.

KEITH: That works for you because you're memorable.

BRIAN: And you aren't?

KEITH: With me they go home and say, what an interesting evening, for years I've heard of idiot savants and now I've met one.

BRIAN: You don't know that.

KEITH: I don't know anything.

BRIAN: In addition to asking questions, you also have to throw back affirmative anecdotes of your own.

KEITH: Oh, sure. Is that all?

BRIAN: All it is, is, "Gee, I know what you mean, something like that happened to me once."

KEITH: Anecdotes? What are you, science fiction? Let's build a robot in the basement with an Erector Set while we're at it. Anecdotes? Your premise would require a scientific miracle.

BRIAN: You do scientific miracles.

KEITH: Yeah, maybe.

BRIAN: Look. Look around you. *(Slapping the furniture)* Where do you think this came from? It's you. It's all you. Huh?

KEITH: I guess I should work this evening.

MICK: *(Offstage)* Ho ho ho! Who's coming down your chimney? (MICK *enters.)* He's got toys for good little girls and boys! *(Turning to* BRIAN) Have you been washing your hands? Mine are clean. (MICK *gives* BRIAN *a little punch. Glancing at* KEITH, *who holds up his hands:)* I know you're spotless. *(Turning back to* BRIAN) Some for you— (MICK *pours microchips into* BRIAN's *hands.)* And some for you. *(He does the same for* KEITH.) And the trucks are at the loading dock.

KEITH: "It came without ribbons! It came without tags! It came without packages, boxes, or bags!"

MICK: You should dispose of this, I think.

(MICK *crosses to the easel, takes a switchblade from his pocket, flicks it open, and slices off the sheet with the writing on it. He puts the sheet on* BRIAN's *desk.*)

KEITH: Wow.

BRIAN: Is that what I think it is?

MICK: *(To* BRIAN*)* Probably not. It's a toy, anymore. *(To* KEITH*)* Want to see?

KEITH: Yeah.

MICK: Souvenir of my good-for-nothing days. Kids today carry automatic weapons. (MICK *closes the knife and flicks it open.*) Like that. You try it.

KEITH: I've never seen a real one. (KEITH *takes the knife and practices with it.*) It's a real one.

BRIAN: Careful, Keith, you need all your fingers.

(BRIAN *gingerly takes the knife and returns it to* MICK, *who closes and pockets it.*)

MICK: Anybody ready for story time?

BRIAN: I am.

MICK: I guarantee you will be happy with this story. I called some people I know.

KEITH: Who?

MICK: It's not important for you to know who. Some people. Totally unconnected, you have no worries. Just a handful of athletes, actually. And their coach. All right?

BRIAN: All right.

MICK: All right, then. I swear to God this is a
kindergarten industry. Now, no one knows for
certain, but if I had to guess, I'd say this is what
happened. A guy calls Prescott's office and says,
"We know where you're dumping your toxic metals.
We have some two-headed babies who want to meet
you, Daddy." And hangs up. Just that. An hour or so
later he gets another call. Different guy. "Your entire
assembly line is about to get homesick for Mexico."
And hangs up. Prescott goes home. It's been a hard
day. In the middle of his dinner there's a knock on the
door. Now you notice all this time there's been
nothing about what anybody wants from him?
He has no idea what's on the horizon. The fellas
told me Prescott opened the little spyhole in the door,
right? And two fellas are standing there. Athletes,
as I said. With their hands in their pockets. And one
of them says, "Mister, why don't you open the door?
It's not that thick." The other fella, this was masterful,
he peers toward the side of the house where the guy
can't see, and he nods, right? Like, "Go around,
everybody." Prescott opens the door in a big hurry.
Moment of truth. I think when all is said and done
he should be grateful. He's learned what he cares for
most. He won't be grateful, they never are. You work,
you do your best—

BRIAN: Prescott opened the door and what happened
to him?

MICK: Something I like to think of as very elegant.
They stand there. Prescott says, "What do you want?"
The man says, "We want to congratulate you. Your
industry, so clean. Your company, so profitable. Your
home, so far from everything." He pulls his hand out
of his pocket. Remember the list of his customers?

BRIAN: Yes.

MICK: The man gave Prescott his list, with a few revisions.

BRIAN: Us and who else?

MICK: That's not important. The point is Prescott took it. Prescott said yes. Prescott said thank you. And the fellas walked away. *(Pause)* A blow is struck for justice and decency, and it won't be traced to us. I was dining with some airtight alibis.

KEITH: Load. Is that great or what?

BRIAN: Congratulations, Mick. You've introduced a whole new way of doing business here.

MICK: It's high time. This is the real world, that's all.

KEITH: Why did you need an alibi?

BRIAN: Extortion is technically speaking illegal.

MICK: A hostile person could give it that construction.

KEITH: A lot of our hobbies fall into the technically illegal category, load.

BRIAN: This is different from toking up, dude. I don't know. It does have a Robin Hood feel to it.

MICK: Rough justice done through nonviolent resistance.

KEITH: Outlaw stuff.

MICK: Now he knows what comes down when you call a person a name.

*(The phone rings. They all look at it. BRIAN picks it up.)*

BRIAN: *(Into phone)* Brian speaking. Hey, Cassius.

KEITH: *(To MICK)* Board member.

*(As BRIAN speaks pleasantly on the phone, he does a broad and expressive mime of pure loathing, to KEITH's vast amusement.)*

BRIAN: We cleared that problem up. You bet. Today, in fact. Well, production's been held up and the quarter ends next week, so I do expect the figures to be down. I'm afraid so. Not as badly as some in the industry. Uh huh. You remember I've been saying for a while that the industry is in a slump? Cassius. There is a difference between an excuse and a valid explanation. Well, if you don't think there is a difference, I say that is admirable of you. Really, that is admirable. That's why I look forward to these calls, Cash. And our board meetings. Two weeks from today, uh huh. But I was saying, you and all the board members, how I value your advice. All these valuable talks. No, thank you. Bye, Cash. See you in two weeks.

(BRIAN *hangs up.*)

MICK: What a shithead.

(BRIAN *belches loudly.*)

BRIAN: Excuse me. Everything I eat now, it ferments down there. Mick?

MICK: Boss?

BRIAN: That's nice. Every executive should have a problem solver.

MICK: Could it be you have a problem?

BRIAN: I have this stomach ache. It's a seasonal thing.

MICK: Is that right?

BRIAN: Every end of quarter. By the time I look around that board room—have you seen our boardroom? With its beautiful deadwood panelling? I look around that board meeting and I try to sit up straight while my guts are lurching from side to side. Most of my concentration goes into not permitting myself to fart. If the board were supportive. If they were fair and good to me.

KEITH: I'd marry them.

BRIAN: We did marry them.

MICK: He's right. And every honeymoon comes to an end. It sucks, but there it is. Would you like me to talk to them?

*(Pause)*

BRIAN: I want you to hurt them and scare them.

MICK: Give me their names. I'll redecorate your boardroom. You like rubber stamp?

BRIAN: Love it.

MICK: And report back to you.

BRIAN: Just the results. Excuse me.

(BRIAN *exits.*)

KEITH: Jeez.

(KEITH *turns to the terminal. Music starts, low then building: Jimi Hendrix's version of* Wild Thing.)

MICK: Don't touch that dial.

KEITH: What?

MICK: Can we talk like people for a minute?

KEITH: For a minute.

(KEITH *pushes a button. The music cuts out.*)

MICK: I appreciate it.

KEITH: That was fabulous.

MICK: Thank you.

KEITH: May I ask a question? You seem to have a very workable substitute for high intelligence.

MICK: All right.

(MICK *picks up a 5-1/4 inch diskette and examines it during the following.*)

KEITH: I may be getting into a sort of *Flowers for Algernon* lifestyle. And I see all these people who are, basically, stupid, and they manage their lives a lot better than I do. How do they do it?

MICK: That's your question. How do stupid people get along.

KEITH: Yeah.

MICK: I wouldn't fucking know, would I?

KEITH: I'm not saying you are one.

MICK: Good.

KEITH: I'm saying you live like one. I've been watching you some.

MICK: I don't like people watching me.

KEITH: So I'm asking. Normal people, then.

MICK: Normal life. What. I have a wife. I have children. Two daughters. You hope they do well. You do your best and pass the baton.

KEITH: Guys my age have little cyberpunk protégés. Everybody's catching up with me.

MICK: That's the time you learn to pay attention.

KEITH: You're, uh, touching the head access hole on my diskette.

MICK: Is that a no-no?

KEITH: *(Retrieving the diskette)* It puts your fingerprints on the memory surface. Mick, you don't actually know shit about computers, do you?

MICK: I'm looking forward to learning.

KEITH: Seriously. You're not even an end user.

MICK: An end user is what?

KEITH: A person who uses pre-programmed software. Our customers.

MICK: So that's an end user. I thought you were asking was I into back door love. What are you doing?

(KEITH *is tapping terminal keys.*)

KEITH: Oh. Sorry, I didn't realize. Well, as long as it's booted up.... Do you know this?

MICK: *(Reading the screen)* "You are standing in a forest clearing." What is this?

KEITH: Sort of a game. What would you do?

MICK: Get the ax, go through the door. So?

(KEITH *looks at* MICK.)

(*Cue up:* Wild Thing)

(*Blackout*)

# ACT TWO

## SCENE 7

*(MICK paces. As he crosses the mood room sensors, music starts and the walls change color. As he crosses back, it changes. He starts to make a game of it, crossing back and forth. Each time, the room responds as if to very different moods.)*

MICK: Pig. *(The walls look like they're boiling. MICK crosses back.)* I've made a place for myself. *(The light grows cooler and more comfortable. He crosses back again.)* I deserve better. *(Ominous shadows grow across the floor.)*

*(BRIAN and KEITH enter.)*

KEITH: Hey, Mick.

MICK: Learning about the new product, here.

BRIAN: *(To KEITH)* Come on, maybe we can jumpstart your head.

KEITH: It's a waste of time.

BRIAN: We can try, what's the harm? Mick, excuse us, Keith and I are doing some brainstorming.

MICK: Great.

*(MICK sits. BRIAN is surprised, but lets it go. He and KEITH assume brainstorming positions.)*

BRIAN: What about the mood room concept?

KEITH: What about it?

BRIAN: I've been sweating over the board meeting, and I got an idea. This room uses one person's input. Expand it! A black box, infinitely adaptable. You know how hard it is with a group of people?

KEITH: Yeah.

BRIAN: Create a place that reflects all the people in it: their characters, their thought, their plots, the way they talk, even music like in here, and visuals, spectacle.

KEITH: Like if our board were meeting, and one of them is about to say something stupid, switchblades could shoot out of the backs of the chairs and impale them.

MICK: Forget them. By the next meeting they'll be a dead issue.

BRIAN: Wouldn't it be cool? If the room were about who was in it?

KEITH: Is this like a Dead concert at all?

BRIAN: Yeah, yeah. But based on people talking. And the room sharing it. Wouldn't that be beautiful?

KEITH: Depending on the people, it could be hell on earth.

BRIAN: A facility that does its own facilitating. Huh? The Consensus Machine!

MICK: When are you planning to put this on the market?

BRIAN: Oh, it's way down the road.

KEITH: Couple of generations.

MICK: What, like your grandchildren?

KEITH: Grandchildren, Jesus, I've got to get a date first.

BRIAN: Generations of technology. Not quite that long. *(To* KEITH*)* But isn't there anything here you could start with?

MICK: I thought this mood room was the next product. So we could tell the chipsters to go to hell.

KEITH: It's not the next product.

BRIAN: It's not the next product per se.

MICK: What is the next product?

BRIAN: This...is what Keith works on while he works on the next product.

KEITH: It's something to do with my hands.

BRIAN: It's a mental stimulus.

KEITH: Relaxation.

BRIAN: Stimulus. Depending.

MICK: What is the next product? If this isn't it?

KEITH: We just got through explaining.

BRIAN: He doesn't like to talk about his concepts.

MICK: You have to talk about your products.

BRIAN: Products, of course, but we're talking about a concept. First we have the idea stage—stop me if I'm wrong—

KEITH: Well, you—

BRIAN: Idea stage, then the concept stage, and finally the product stage. Keith's in an ideational-conceptual flux right now.

MICK: The part he won't talk about.

BRIAN: Right.

MICK: So when are we going to have something to sell?

KEITH: Ideas come when they come. All I can do is squeeze a bit.

MICK: Hadn't you better squeeze a little harder?

KEITH: I'm not a hermit. I'm aware of the calendar.

MICK: What you're saying is, the pipeline's dry.

KEITH: I need those dilithium crystals, Mister Scott! Captain, I canna keep the matter and the antimatter from colliding!

*(Pause)*

MICK: Does the board know about this?

BRIAN: No reason they should. It's not their business yet.

MICK: I'd better tell you what's going down with them.

BRIAN: Just the results.

MICK: I am talking about who owns you.

BRIAN: I have to deal with this.

*(Pause)*

MICK: So, Keith. You need to make up an idea?

KEITH: They're out there, you feel your way around until you bump into one.

MICK: Sounds easy enough, just move your mind around, why don't I go be a genius? Huh?

KEITH: Almost everyone never moves.

MICK: I'm going to do some brainstorming myself.

BRIAN: Mick, this is not the way we do this.

KEITH: Artoo. Let the Wookie win.

MICK: Okay. You know what I don't get about this mood room? Why do you want a room that tells people what you're thinking?

BRIAN: It's supposed to set the dominant tone.

MICK: That doesn't need a machine. You'd never make a profit. Now, everyone would buy a machine that tells them what other people are thinking.

KEITH: This technology won't do that.

MICK: What will it do?

KEITH: At most it'll tell you more or less how they're feeling.

MICK: Anybody worth his salt sitting with someone knows how they're feeling—body language, eye contact, tone of voice.

KEITH: No kidding. What I wouldn't give. "I have one word to say to you, Benjamin."

BRIAN: Yes, Sir?

KEITH: Women.

MICK: Right, and another thing—

BRIAN: You can stop now, Mick. There is no other thing. You've got him.

MICK: Are there any other guys like you out there?

KEITH: We know a lot of them.

MICK: Okay, then we've got customers. Recording emotional states—you know, I bet we could nail down a defense contract? Make a portable model. A few refinements—we could make the whole idea of the "business" meeting obsolete. Then we're in a position to sell the product to counteract it.

BRIAN: *(Grudging)* A mind-tapping device?

MICK: Catchy. I like it. Lie-detectors are way too crude, wires and shit hang all over you, throw off the results.

KEITH: Hardware in the way.

BRIAN: The legal implications alone are staggering.

MICK: Great, huh? This could be a major service. People could really get to know each other better. Why didn't you guys come up with this? It's perfect.

BRIAN: I was concentrating on my...Consensus Machine idea.

MICK: Which, as I said, I don't see how anybody's going to want. You guys, I don't know, you get a problem, the first thing you think is maybe a machine can fix it for us.

BRIAN: Machines are how people want us to think. They put us on the map.

MICK: Could a machine get your chips? Could a machine go after your board?

BRIAN: You're talking about the outside world; we're talking electronics.

MICK: Believe me, I see the temptation. We sit here, nice and cool, handling ideas. This is fine. I'm into this. What? *(This last to* KEITH, *who is staring in his direction, transfixed.* BRIAN *beams.)* Are you pretending there's something in back of me? What's the joke?

BRIAN: Shh. There's nothing in back of you. Come on.

MICK: Can't he ever just adjourn a meeting?

BRIAN: Don't spook him.

MICK: Spook him, what is he, a game animal? What's going on?

*(*BRIAN *pulls* MICK *out the door.)*

KEITH: Could a machine get your— Could a machine
go after your— *(Pause)* This is pathetically old.
Very ugly. *(Pause)* It comes in looking useful.
It needs a weakness. So, something useful...needs
a weakness.... It joins the system and becomes the
system. So, useful...weakness...becomes the system....
Time. It has to work in time. It has to work in the
world of matter. *(Pause)* It's an idea. *(Pause)* And
that's why I'm the incorporated boy!

*(Van Halen's* You Really Got Me)

*(Blackout)*

## SCENE 8

*(Night.* MICK *is looking through file drawers.* KEITH *peeks
in.)*

KEITH: What are you doing here?

MICK: What are you doing here?

KEITH: I've taken up pacing. You're not in your office.

MICK: People pace, they pace back and forth.

KEITH: My pacing describes a complex polygon
through the corridors and the assembly floor.
Linear pacing would hardly be appropriate.

MICK: You're working.

KEITH: I'm trying to. The programming's gonna be the
easy part. What are you doing?

MICK: Working.

KEITH: At two a.m.?

MICK: I've been working day and night. You see me
working today?

KEITH: Yes.

MICK: Now I'm working tonight. Some kinds of work demand privacy.

KEITH: Like what?

MICK: Research.

KEITH: Does Brian know about your research?

MICK: Brian has given me carte blanche. Wouldn't you say? About this, no.

KEITH: I had a feeling.

MICK: If anything comes of it, it'll be a surprise. So talk to me. About Brian.

KEITH: Brian is trying everyth—

MICK: —everything. I've heard that.

KEITH: He's been the managing director since we started. He's always been very good to me.

MICK: I agree that that has been true. And I would say that he has worked well.

KEITH: Yes, look at how much we've grown.

MICK: Which may be the reason he's saying these things.

KEITH: What things?

MICK: Listen to him. Every other sentence out of his mouth is "I don't know." The man sits there and says, "I don't know what to do." No man in a leadership position has the right to say that. Not in front of employees.

KEITH: He trusts me. We go back so far.

MICK: And me? What's his excuse for trusting me that far?

KEITH: He trusts you, too.

MICK: No, he does not. He does not trust me.

KEITH: How can you tell?

MICK: A dozen little ways.

KEITH: Like what? I'm trying to learn these things.

MICK: He's trying to learn. This is not school.

KEITH: I hated school.

MICK: Is that so.

KEITH: They make you do everything 1, 2, 3, 4, 5, 6, 7, 8. Which I guess is an okay way to teach old ideas, but if you're trying to find new ones you've got to go 1, 2, 3, 4, Q, H, elephant, 12, ukelele, St. Ambrose. You know?

MICK: All right.

KEITH: I want to start learning out in the world. Out of doors?

MICK: Tell you what. You watch Brian. Try and spot the ways he doesn't trust me. Later we'll have a quiz.

KEITH: Interesting.

MICK: See, my feeling is he's unhappy.

KEITH: You think?

MICK: I think he's miserable. He doesn't want to be doing this. You can see it.

KEITH: Can you?

MICK: You'd think no one had ever called his bluff before. A breath of wind and down he goes.

KEITH: Like data. Get a bit of dust in one of your drives and you're gone.

MICK: That's it. He's got dust in his drives.

KEITH: I've always thought of human beings as these great lumpy solid unknowable big-as-life inevitabilities. Rocks. Hard places.

MICK: They mostly fold up as soon as you touch them. My daughters. They're lying around the floor in front of the T.V., it's time for bed, all I have to do is walk heavy across the floor, real slow—

KEITH: Creature from the Black Lagoon.

MICK: All right. With the hands out, and they start giggling. Don't tickle me! Don't tickle me! And I go, I haven't touched you. They're screaming, you're going to, you're going to! The closer I get, the more they're laughing, I still haven't touched them and they're off like out of a doublebarrel shotgun up the stairs, down the hall, into bed, still laughing. Brian's the same, I get up from my chair and he's in bed with the covers over his head.

KEITH: I used to hide under the covers with a flashlight, so my parents wouldn't know I was reading science fiction all night. I was still into hard media back then.

MICK: Hiding? What are you telling me?

KEITH: What? Nothing.

MICK: You've made me think.

KEITH: Your daughters are going to hate me.

MICK: Don't worry about my daughters.

(Blackout)

(Instrumental break from Yes's Roundabout)


**SCENE 9**


(BRIAN and KEITH, very serious)

KEITH: Don't be too hard on him, okay?

BRIAN: We need to discuss a couple of things. Keith, if you'd rather not stay—

KEITH: I want to. You want to go out tonight? Do some 'shrooms and go to the Giants game?

(MICK *enters.*)

MICK: You called? Have you read your mail?

BRIAN: I think I've mentioned I'm not big into paper.

MICK: If you read your mail, I believe you'll see the resignations of at least two of your board members.

BRIAN: Resignations? My God.

MICK: You're welcome.

BRIAN: Resignations? I thought you were just going to bring them into line.

MICK: Into line or out of the picture.

BRIAN: My God. Which board members?

MICK: I don't know which ones, I don't read your mail.

BRIAN: You don't know which ones? You're expecting more? What are you doing to them?

MICK: You only wanted to know results.

BRIAN: You have to back off them.

MICK: Bad timing. I just started fucking with them, I pull out now everyone gets frustrated.

BRIAN: A corporation is required to have somebody on its board. It's a law.

MICK: I know some investors. I've told them about this company. They're eager to get into a growth area.

(*Pause*)

BRIAN: So that's how it's done.

MICK: What did you want to see me about?

BRIAN: I called the chip company.

MICK: Hey. If there's a problem with the chip company, I'll call the guy.

BRIAN: There's a problem with the chip company.

MICK: Okay, what?

BRIAN: Prescott. Your contact. He resigned.

KEITH: Good-bye, Mr. Chips.

MICK: Nobody in this business stands up to heat, do they?

BRIAN: He was one of the original guys.

KEITH: Poor scumbag.

MICK: Have they hired a replacement?

BRIAN: Yes. He's cut off our chip supply.

*(Pause)*

MICK: What's his name?

BRIAN: We can't keep doing this.

MICK: Why not?

BRIAN: There'll be nobody left!

MICK: So what? All that's important is we get chips and keep producing.

BRIAN: No board, no colleagues. We're back where we started. This industry eats you by degrees.

MICK: So what's the new guy's name? My investors are not going to go for this situation.

BRIAN: I'd like to hear more about these investors.

MICK: I'll tell you what you need to know, what are we going to do, turn them down? We're not in that position.

BRIAN: Are they people from—your industry?

MICK: What is it about me—you don't trust me?

BRIAN: Why do you think I don't trust you?

MICK: You're asking me questions all the time.

BRIAN: To find out what you're doing.

MICK: Why do you want to do that?

BRIAN: What are you talking about? I'm your boss.

MICK: Oh, well. Oh, well then. As long as you're in charge. You tell me what you want me to do. I'll do those things.

BRIAN: I don't want to work like that.

MICK: Have you checked out my background? *(Pause)* I know you haven't, because if you had checked my background you wouldn't be asking this type of question all the time. Check me out.

BRIAN: Nah, nah. It's all right.

MICK: Check me out. You know how wearing this is on me? I'm a right guy.

BRIAN: I believe you.

MICK: No you don't. I've got references.

BRIAN: It's all right.

MICK: Since when is my history an issue? Anybody here into making my history an issue? If you don't know who I am by now, and you're employing me, that is your fault.

BRIAN: It's all my fault, I see what's shaping up.

MICK: Do you want me to submit a resignation?

BRIAN: Nobody wants that.

MICK: Nobody wants that? You don't want that.
Me, I'm not so sure. I know there's no jobs out there
for a white man with demands. I also know some
things in life are not worth the money we're talking
about when we're talking salary. And one of those
things is to be treated with mistrust by a person in
no position. No position.

BRIAN: Mick, you think I mean something when lots
of times I don't.

*(Outside the window, the sky is darkening.)*

MICK: What do you think I am? You think you can
drop the soap and I'll bend right over? You want
me to help you bring down the board. I like it. You're
trying to turn and fight. But if I took off and left you
to fight alone, what would happen to you?

*(There is a huge crash of thunder.)*

BRIAN: What the fuck?

MICK: Jesus, look out there. I've never seen a storm
like this in California.

KEITH: It's not in California, it's in the window. It's a
projection.

MICK: Where do you get these ideas?

KEITH: Shakespeare. Right? Brian? That arts center we
gave the grant to.

BRIAN: We saw a play. The king gets upset, it starts to
rain, Keith liked it.

KEITH: That and "Lonely Teardrops". Jackie Wilson,
Shakespeare, it all adds up.

MICK: Doesn't anything in this room have any
connection with the real world? *(To KEITH)* Hey.
Are you getting any of this?

(KEITH *looks at the wind and the rain.*)

KEITH: I'm starting to. Brian, how about if Mick goes to talk to the clown. Just talk. I'll go along. Huh? I won't get in the way. I'll learn a lot. Mick?

MICK: *(To* KEITH*)* You want to go on a field trip? *(To* BRIAN*)* Sure, sign his permission slip, let him go.

(MICK *exits.*)

BRIAN: I don't think he's really mad. That's how he negotiates.

KEITH: Negotiating is hard, huh?

*(Pause)*

BRIAN: So you're gonna scream. This is too funny.

KEITH: What, tell me.

BRIAN: You ready? I went to the doctor. I have an ulcer.

KEITH: Oh.

BRIAN: Yeah.

KEITH: An ulcer? You?

BRIAN: Can you believe it?

KEITH: But I thought mostly people who got those were, like—

BRIAN: Middle-aged businessmen. It turns out lots of people can get them. All walks of life. But mostly they're middle-aged businessmen.

KEITH: Not boyish happy-go-lucky businessmen?

BRIAN: My father had an ulcer!

KEITH: This sucks, Brian. So what happens? Lots of milk and, like, plain yoghurt?

BRIAN: Yeesh. Plain yoghurt.

KEITH: Yeesh. That stuff is like Cup o' Sperm.

BRIAN: Don't try to cheer me up. Oh, and listen to this: The doctor says, "Have you considered slowing down?"

*(They laugh.)*

KEITH: Slowing down? How does that work? *(like a phonograph record, winding down)* Hel-lo, my name is Bri-an Weiss. I'm in the com-pu-ter in...dus...try....

*(KEITH laughs. BRIAN swallows painfully.)*

BRIAN: Ow!

KEITH: Puh-lease. Maestro, the violins.

BRIAN: If I had anything else, you wouldn't laugh at me.

KEITH: If you had a hernia I'd laugh at you. Come on. All those middle-aged businessmen, they never slow down, do they? Do they? Your father never did slow down.

BRIAN: My father was a workaholic hustle artist with major vices.

KEITH: Oh, so it's a whole different thing.

BRIAN: Hey. Don't get too fucking insightful all at once, okay? People might start to expect something from you.

KEITH: Try lightening up, load.

BRIAN: You. You have done this to me. You!

KEITH: Ladies and gentlemen: The ulcerizer!

BRIAN: It slices. It dices. *(KEITH air-guitars his way toward the computer.)* Hey. Can we think mellow thoughts for a moment? I want to hear a slow tune.

*(Pink Floyd's* Wish You Were Here. *Blackout)*

## SCENE 10

(BRIAN *is wearing a suit, and is finishing tying his tie.*
MICK *enters.*)

MICK: They're all waiting. Aren't you gonna come?

BRIAN: Sure I'm gonna come.

MICK: Want me to walk down with you?

BRIAN: That's okay.

MICK: They haven't told me when they want my
presentation. *(Pause)* Where's Keith? Is he coming?

BRIAN: Your presentation?

MICK: Yeah. They didn't even tell you?

BRIAN: *(Casually)* No, why should they?

MICK: What a bunch of shitheads.

(KEITH *enters, wearing a suit, dress shirt, and new cowboy
boots. His necktie is untied.*)

KEITH: Okay. Listen. We get through the meeting, we
ditch the board, we drive to my house and play some
metal? Do some sixes? How about it? *(KEITH attempts
to tie his tie.)* There's this woman in Marketing. Do you
think.... Could you invite her for me? Brian?

BRIAN: We'll see.

KEITH: Where were you this afternoon, man? How do
I look?

BRIAN: Don't hang yourself, there.

KEITH: I wasn't sure about the boots.

BRIAN: Very corporate.

KEITH: So where were you?

MICK: People were asking.

BRIAN: *(To* MICK*)* We have some investments in alternative energy tax shelters. *(To* KEITH*)* Remember our windmills?

KEITH: Oh yeah. I've never seen them.

BRIAN: Neither had I. So I took a drive up to Altamont Pass and had a look.

(KEITH *pulls off the tie and holds it out to* BRIAN.)

KEITH: This is broken.

BRIAN: Give it. (BRIAN *puts the tie around his neck and knots it.)* It's spooky up there, you know? Thousands of windmills, all over the hills. They aren't little Dutch boy stuff, they're like—remember in one of the *Planet of the Apes* movies, the acres of crucified chimpanzees?

KEITH: Yeah.

BRIAN: Replace chimpanzees with airplane engines. They look like propeller motors on poles. Not going anywhere. Hills full of hardware. They all face the same way, wherever the wind left them last. They're standing out there waving. "I am Spartacus." "I am Spartacus."

KEITH: What's that from?

BRIAN: *Spartacus.* Duh. A movie. Kubrick. *2001*?

KEITH: Him.

BRIAN: Yeah. Some of them, their arm things are tied down. Their depreciation's all used up. The wind blows through the pass, but no one wants them making power anymore.

KEITH: Visiting windmills in business hours. You've gotten quixotic.

MICK: You want me to tell them to start without you?

BRIAN: We're coming.

(BRIAN *loosens the necktie, pulls it up over his head, and puts it over* KEITH's, *tightening it around his neck and straightening it for him during:*)

KEITH: Someone told me these boots cost three hundred dollars. Isn't that incredible? Remember when we had three hundred dollars between us?

BRIAN: It was two-hundred eighty and yes, I do.

KEITH: Three-hundred dollars. How can that possibly be? Golden cows?

BRIAN: They look like eelskin, Keith.

KEITH: Really? They are supple. Perfect for a board meeting. My feet want to snake through the murky depths!

(*They exit.*)

(*Blackout*)

(*Muddy Waters's* Mannish Boy)

## SCENE 11

(BRIAN *slams the door open and stalks in.* KEITH *follows him in and closes the door.*)

BRIAN: How dare they ask me questions like that? After all these years?

KEITH: Because they wanted the answers?

BRIAN: They knew the answers! Since when are they so fucking well-informed? I've been telling them for a year and a half there's a shakeout going on.

KEITH: So they finally heard you.

(BRIAN *searches through his desk drawers until he finds a bottle of Maalox.*)

BRIAN: Not me. It's not me they're hearing.

(BRIAN *takes a swig from the Maalox bottle. He takes several more in the next few minutes.)*

KEITH: It sure isn't me.

BRIAN: No, it sure isn't. They were all looking at you. They were all waiting on you for a word.

KEITH: On me?

BRIAN: Yes.

KEITH: What for?

BRIAN: Keith, you're the franchise.

KEITH: We're the franchise, load.

BRIAN: They're coming in on us. The fast operators are rising around our necks.

KEITH: Fuck 'em.

BRIAN: Why didn't you say that during the meeting?

KEITH: You worked with me for years not to say "fuck" in board meetings. Those minutes are public record.

BRIAN: They were all waiting for you to put in a good word for me.

KEITH: Nobody told me that.

BRIAN: Couldn't you sense it? The room reeked.

KEITH: What are you talking about? I don't understand what you're talking about anymore, dude. They prepared some questions, big deal.

BRIAN: Didn't that strike you as unusual?

KEITH: They've never done it before, if that's what you mean.

BRIAN: That's what I'm getting at, yeah.

KEITH: Isn't that their right?

BRIAN: What?

KEITH: I don't know anything about this. Let's get wasted, huh?

BRIAN: Later. What did you mean?

KEITH: When?

BRIAN: About their asking questions.

KEITH: All those months during the start-up, when you were dragging me to these meetings and making me stand up and talk about my ideas—I've almost gotten used to that now, you know? Don't you think I'm getting more natural?

BRIAN: Much. Almost lifelike.

KEITH: Back then you told me the stockholders own the company. That's why we got all that stock when we went public. And the board answers to the stockholders, right? Like they're elected and stuff.

BRIAN: Right.

KEITH: Dude! I'm getting this straight. Okay, so if they have all these stockholders to answer to, don't they need a few answers?

BRIAN: That's why we have these meetings, asshole.

KEITH: My point exactly, anus-brain.

BRIAN: Don't you get what I'm saying? (BRIAN *goes to drink from the Maalox, finds it's empty, and throws it away.*) It's not that they're asking questions. If they want to ask questions, like you say, that's their right. Hell, we're stockholders, they're protecting our investment. But don't you see what they're doing?

KEITH: Goddamn it, Brian, if I could figure out what fucking people were doing I wouldn't have hooked

up with you in the first place! Would I? That's what
I've needed you for.

*(*BRIAN *holds his stomach, swallows painfully, swallows
again, and gags.* KEITH *rushes for the trashcan and holds
it under* BRIAN*'s chin.)*

BRIAN: They think they're protecting our investment
from me.

KEITH: Really?

BRIAN: *(Hugging the trash can)* It's not that they're
asking questions. It's that they prepared questions
out of the blue sky, without giving me a chance to
prepare thorough answers, and when I told them that
the answers aren't exact, they wanted to know why,
and then they asked if I couldn't just be a little more
specific, and then I tried to be more specific, and
then they brought out those sheets of figures that
contradicted what I said, and they said they had
these figures prepared that seem not to agree with
my contentions, and I say that I told them my figures
were approximate, and that I would be happy to
prepare a thorough set of figures for the next
Treasurer's Committee meeting, and they say that
won't be necessary, they have these figures already,
and if they have the figures already, why the fuck
were they asking? Clearly they weren't going to trust
my answers. They walk in thinking I'm going to
screw up, and then they screw me up. Didn't you
notice that?

KEITH: Which?

BRIAN: Didn't you notice me getting crucified in there?

KEITH: I was looking at the figures.

BRIAN: You were looking at the figures. Of course you
were. You were looking so close at the figures you
didn't see what was happening to the humans in the

room. You were looking so close at the fucking figures that when a friend needed your help the whole thing passed you by.

KEITH: You needed my help? At a meeting?

BRIAN: Yes!

KEITH: What kind of help was I supposed to give you?

BRIAN: You were supposed to say, if your figures and Brian's figures disagree, then there must be something wrong with your figures.

KEITH: How would I know that?

BRIAN: Or you could have said, if you have questions for the management, please let us know. We'll get those answers to you. Us, get it? Identifying yourself with me.

KEITH: But you were answering their questions.

BRIAN: Because I didn't have a choice! Nobody pulled me out of the fire! And I screwed up! Or you could have seen me screwing up and said, I don't feel comfortable with the tone of these questions. I would feel more comfortable if you would reconsider your approach to this issue.

KEITH: This is me saying this.

BRIAN: Why not?

KEITH: Because I've never said anything like that in my life!

BRIAN: Maybe it's time you start. Maybe it's time you get some grasp of the politics around here.

KEITH: You want a politician, you know you've got the wrong boy.

BRIAN: It's going to be like this from here on. Not to mention what'll happen when Mick gets his investors in the door. We should have stuck together in there. You could have backed me up when Mick started in.

KEITH: I backed you up to everyone in sight the last week.

BRIAN: Hold the phone. Did you know this was coming down on me?

KEITH: Didn't you?

BRIAN: Of course not.

KEITH: Just about every board member called me up.

BRIAN: And you didn't tell me.

KEITH: What was I supposed to—Danger, Will Robinson! Danger, danger! I thought whatever I was hearing, you had to know already. I'm always the last to hear, you know me.

BRIAN: I guess I'm out of the loop.

KEITH: And I was p.o.'d you hadn't told me the situation.

BRIAN: I didn't know the situation. I don't know this place anymore.

KEITH: And we worked so hard to get here. The big time.

BRIAN: What?

KEITH: Well. We're big time. We can't hide it.

BRIAN: Well. Maybe I'm just not ready for the big time.

KEITH: Maybe not.

BRIAN: What?

KEITH: Maybe you're not ready for the big time. This is making you so unhappy.

BRIAN: Load, that's not what you're supposed to say.

KEITH: Look—

BRIAN: You're supposed to say, of course you're ready for the big time, they're not ready for you. Nitpicking scumbags.

KEITH: Look—

BRIAN: You're supposed to—

KEITH: Stop telling me what I'm supposed to fucking say!

BRIAN: You're supposed to comfort me a little.

KEITH: Oh, sure. Manners.

BRIAN: We're supposed to be these grown men now.

KEITH: I didn't become your partner in order to be a grownup.

BRIAN: That was a long time ago.

KEITH: *(Pointing to the terminal)* And don't tell me about the passage of time. I know all about it. You know what this is? It's a jalopy. It's a quaint device.

BRIAN: I thought it was the state of the art.

KEITH: State of the art is a jalopy. In the time it takes to screw it together, it's antiquated. In the time it takes to think it up. Before I think this thought again, I'll see a picture of this console and it'll look like '70s lapels. Look at that bloat! Did we start it with a crank? Remember the old movie from—what, the '30s?— seventh-grade social studies, General Motors's City of the Future. "Our monorail passes over peaceful avenues. But why are there no slums? Why is there no grime? Because this is the world of 1960!" We're living in stupid history.

BRIAN: We're the ones thinking into the future.

KEITH: For a while. Flying on ideas. I'm like a jet engine: Something comes to me, I take it in, the next second I blow it out my ass, the only way to stay up. That's what inspiration means.

BRIAN: What are you saying?

KEITH: All around us, our generation of nerds, like the battery commercial, right? The toys are flying, which one has the Duracell? Here goes another one, crash and burn. This is where we are. Left behind in the City of the Future.

BRIAN: Come on. This room is full of beautiful thinking.

KEITH: Mick is right. Some things are not for the marketplace.

BRIAN: And you're working on a new idea.

KEITH: It's rotten, this idea. It's like digging up a corpse. I'm watching my brain walk out of Shangri-La. It's all—old in here. I'm sorry. You've done all you could.

BRIAN: This is it, then. I always knew this day would come. *(Pause)* Here's what we do. Do you think you can finish this idea?

KEITH: Do I have to? If you say so. I can try.

BRIAN: That's my boy. So I'll go first, then.

KEITH: Wait. You're leaving me here?

BRIAN: We can't both leave at once, the stock will fall down a hole. We can't do that to the employees.

KEITH: We'll lose all our Dungeons and Dragons players.

BRIAN: We go one at a time, maybe the market won't notice. Okay? Come on, don't be scared.

KEITH: Okay. Listen! You want to set up a game Friday night?

BRIAN: Yes. Excellent.

KEITH: Brian! Hey! The next sound you hear will be a heavy weight lifting off your shoulders. Right? Am I right?

BRIAN: You're right. You know? You're right.

*(The lights fade.)*

*(Led Zeppelin's* Going to California*)*

## SCENE 12

*(MICK enters. He carries a little bundle of mail with a rubber band around it. KEITH follows him in.)*

MICK: I'm telling this new clown the same as I told Prescott, it's getting me nowhere, I look around, you've wandered away.

KEITH: I wore the suit, didn't I?

MICK: What did Brian do with you, keep you on a leash? I look all over Mnemonico, you're playing with somebody's terminal.

*(As he talks, MICK casually flicks out his switchblade and slits open his mail.)*

KEITH: What time is it?

MICK: Ten minutes to four. Listen, we have to talk. You and I, we've talked about things we could do together. New ideas.

KEITH: Yes.

MICK: The board has this executive search committee. They're going to call you.

KEITH: About what?

MICK: About our plans. Yours and mine. Then they'll let us go ahead.

KEITH: They've always let me go ahead.

MICK: That's it. You talk to them, and they let us go ahead.

KEITH: Oh, us!

MICK: Us. All right?

KEITH: Great! Hang on, I can work this out. They want to know about us. They want to know what I think about us.

MICK: All right?

KEITH: They know what I think about me. So they want to know what I think about you. Right? See, I'm catching on!

MICK: I've been Brian's problem-solver. Getting your chips for you, clearing out your board. So, since Brian resigned—

KEITH: What time is it?

MICK: Nine minutes to four. Why?

KEITH: Have to see if my idea works. Four o'clock, let me know.

MICK: This is important. You're the brain trust. They need to know how well we work together.

KEITH: Cassius called me. So that's what that was.

MICK: What did you say?

KEITH: I said you have a lot to offer. You have new ideas all the time. You get things done.

MICK: Thank you. What else?

KEITH: He said you'd been telling him about that Mind-Tapping—

MICK: The Mind-Tapping Device? He asked about that? Great, that really hooked 'em.

KEITH: So I had to explain that it won't work. And then a couple of the other board members called and I had to explain to them, which took up more time.

MICK: What do you mean, it won't work?

KEITH: It'll take five years minimum R and D and way beyond that to the marketplace. We all agreed it's an unworkable, ignorant, cockamamie, fascistic concept. But that it wasn't a reflection on your character. I told them I've learned a lot from you, so I said we'd just have to find a way around the fact that you're illiterate.

MICK: I've got a fucking M.B.A.

KEITH: Computer illiterate. I told them how fast you catch onto things, but by then they were all saying the last thing we need is someone who doesn't know computers.

MICK: I'll pick it up.

KEITH: They're not talking about your learning to be an end user. The board is saying you don't know what computers mean. Like your idea. It's a false turn, a dead end. So they think you don't know where you are. Technologically.

(MICK *quickly shuffles through his mail and finds the envelope he's looking for.*)

MICK: Shit. (MICK *takes out a letter. A pause while he reads.*) They've rolled my head. I don't get it. They know better.

KEITH: They fired you?

MICK: They don't know about computers, either. That's no reason. There is nothing you can do with that thing that I can't do walking around. What do they think, they can write me a letter and I'll go away?

KEITH: You won't?

MICK: No. I'll make them change their minds. Or I'll bring in people with other ideas. So the question is, who did this to me? Keith, help me here.

KEITH: If I can, how?

MICK: Think back to the conversations. Whose idea was this? I want his name. Think!

*(Pause)*

KEITH: It's not important for you to know that.

*(Pause)*

MICK: What is that supposed to mean?

KEITH: It's what you say.

MICK: It's what I say when I've jammed it to somebody!

KEITH: Like Brian?

MICK: Brian resigned. *(Pause)* And nobody stopped it. You didn't stop him. *(Pause)* You used me.

KEITH: You were right. He was unhappy.

MICK: I turned your board against him. You let me engineer it.

KEITH: You know how I am. I'm so vague about politics.

MICK: You and him stay pals. And I'm out. When did you get so goddamn calculating?

KEITH: It's not important for you to know that.

MICK: I say that! Stop quoting me! You used me like I was some putz. Some stupid dickhead.

KEITH: Yes, well, one uses one's dick. One doesn't let it run one's life.

MICK: I can't let you do this!

KEITH: I'm not negotiating. You don't have to pretend to be angry.

MICK: This is real! This is real! (MICK *means his anger, but he's pointing his switchblade for emphasis.* KEITH's *eyes widen in panic.* MICK, *confused, follows* KEITH's *gaze. They both look at the knife.*) What? (KEITH *shoots out one hand and grabs* MICK's *wrist. They stand like that.*) Brian said you had reflexes. That's not my joystick, boy.

KEITH: I was never into sports. I'm a physical coward, it's no secret to me.

MICK: I'm not fighting you. If we were fighting, I'd do this. (MICK *quickly reaches for the switchblade with his other hand. Just as quickly* KEITH *grabs that wrist with his free hand.* KEITH *is holding one of* MICK's *wrists in each hand. They are facing each other.*) Shall we dance?

KEITH: *(Almost babbling)* Do you really think this would be the best thing to do, killing me? I'm debating some pluses and minuses.

MICK: Listen! We are not fighting. I want to work for you.

KEITH: The computer business is getting strange. They have me heavily insured. They'd never pay, of course. You'd have executives knifing each other all over the country. No one would get any work done.

MICK: Listen to me! You got me a little pissed, okay? I'll forget it if you'll forget it. In business these things happen all the time. Don't you see how bad you need me? I can tell you about real life. I've got investors. I'm on your side. You don't know what I can do.

KEITH: I know I don't.

*(Suddenly the knife is very close to* KEITH.*)*

MICK: How did you get to know so fucking much?! Huh?!

KEITH: The mood room.

MICK: What about it?

KEITH: Everything here is input. It's been recording you.

MICK: You've been recording me?

KEITH: The room has. That's how it works.

MICK: You've had me bugged?

KEITH: Not me. The room.

MICK: I'll put down the knife.

*(*MICK *lets go of the knife.* KEITH *puts his foot on it and lets go of* MICK.*)*

KEITH: *(With growing hysteria)* The room has your input. I have your numbers! I've gotten to your whole life through that terminal. Didn't you know you're in here? The network never forgets. It's all in there, all your numbers. Your convict number.

MICK: You checked up on me.

KEITH: You said to! You've been programmed. If anything happens to me, if you call anyone in this industry, you go back to prison automatically. And then you will vanish from memory. Even your daughters will forget you. I can crunch your numbers!

*(*KEITH's *hand is poised over the keyboard.*)*

MICK: I would work hard for you. You'd know all about me.

KEITH: What time is it?

MICK: Four.

KEITH: Shit! What's the chip guy's name again?

(KEITH *grabs the phone and punches a number, referring to the palm of his hand where it's written in pen.*)

MICK: Ziegler. Are you calling him?

KEITH: *(To* MICK*)* Not really. *(Into phone)* Hi, is Mr. Ziegler in? This is Keith Rienzi. Well, thanks, I'm flattered. No, that's always nice to hear. What? Uh huh? What, just now? While we were talking? God, really. What's on the monitor? On all of them? Somebody better shut your system down fast. Sure, I can hold.

MICK: What's going on?

(KEITH *opens a desk drawer, reaches deep inside it, and takes out a large folded piece of paper during:*)

KEITH: Hi. Tell you what, we know something about this stuff, maybe we can help. Have Mr. Ziegler call me right away. No, I want to talk to him in particular. You're welcome. (KEITH *hangs up. He crosses to hang the piece of paper on the easel. It is* MICK's *list of options.*) Everything you know is being recreated in electronics. It's the next frontier.

(KEITH *picks up a felt pen and circles* "Sabotage.")

MICK: Sabotage.

KEITH: And I'm the fastest man there. While you met with Ziegler, I input a time-activated—screw it. Why am I wasting my energy saying this into the air? Air's got no memory. *(The phone rings.* KEITH *and* MICK *look at each other for a moment.)* You've done your job. You can go now. (KEITH *picks up the phone.* MICK *exits.)* Keith Rienzi. Hi, Mr. Ziegler. Larry. Hi. I hear your computers are doing funny things. Yeah. It's good you came to me. I bet my people could help you. I could do it personally. The hackers call it a

virus. Now if I do this as a favor to you, I hope that
chip shortage will get cleared up.  Well. The minute I
have those chips, I'm on my way over. Oh, great. That
is good news. Now listen to me carefully. I'll clear up
your virus, the hackers come up with new stuff every
day. We're thinking of marketing our knowhow.
It would be a service, we'd be providing a service—
*(Trying to think of a catchy word)* Protection. Yeah.
Send the trucks. *(*KEITH *punches another line button.)*
Software boys? It's Keith. Get your booties up here,
I'm picking protégés. Warp factor nine, Mr. Chekhov!
*(*KEITH *slams his fist onto his desk. Rolling Stones's*
Jumping Jack Flash *starts up. The walls go blood red.*
*Through the window streams a sunset like fire.* KEITH
*considers what his room is telling him. He punches*
*numbers.)* This is Keith Rienzi. Fix me up a new office.
A man can't hear himself think in here. *(*KEITH *hangs*
*up and takes it all in.)* Oh yeah?! Oh yeah?!

*(He air-guitars savagely.)*

*(Blackout)*